# REBORN
## A TRUE STORY OF LIFE AND DEATH

FELI MERCADO

**BALBOA.**PRESS
A DIVISION OF HAY HOUSE

Copyright © 2022 Feli Mercado.

All rights reserved. No part of this book may be used or reproduced by any means, graphic, electronic, or mechanical, including photocopying, recording, taping or by any information storage retrieval system without the written permission of the author except in the case of brief quotations embodied in critical articles and reviews.

Balboa Press books may be ordered through booksellers or by contacting:

Balboa Press
A Division of Hay House
1663 Liberty Drive
Bloomington, IN 47403
www.balboapress.com
844-682-1282

Because of the dynamic nature of the Internet, any web addresses or links contained in this book may have changed since publication and may no longer be valid. The views expressed in this work are solely those of the author and do not necessarily reflect the views of the publisher, and the publisher hereby disclaims any responsibility for them.

The author of this book does not dispense medical advice or prescribe the use of any technique as a form of treatment for physical, emotional, or medical problems without the advice of a physician, either directly or indirectly. The intent of the author is only to offer information of a general nature to help you in your quest for emotional and spiritual well-being. In the event you use any of the information in this book for yourself, which is your constitutional right, the author and the publisher assume no responsibility for your actions.

Any people depicted in stock imagery provided by Getty Images are models, and such images are being used for illustrative purposes only.
Certain stock imagery © Getty Images.

Print information available on the last page.

ISBN: 979-8-7652-3045-9 (sc)
ISBN: 979-8-7652-3040-4 (e)

Balboa Press rev. date: 06/24/2022

# AUTHOR'S NOTES

- **Reborn** – *A True Story of Life & Death* was originally published in Spanish (*May 2022*) as **Life and Death**. The English version was edited for publication by California author, journalist and poet John Aiello, who also contributed an original poem for this manuscript published in Chapter XIV.

- **This work depicts actual events in the life of the author as truthfully as recollection permits**. While all persons within are actual individuals, names and identifying characteristics have been changed to respect their privacy.

- This book presents an original memoir by Feli Mercado and the story and its description belong solely to her. All factual representations made and all opinions shared reflect her work product and not the work product of her editor, whose sole responsibilities for this project were editorial: checking the manuscript for logic and syntax; and placing it in the proper format for the genre.

# CONTENTS

Preface ..................................................................................xiii

| | | |
|---|---|---|
| I | An Encounter With Reality................................................1 |
| II | The Diagnosis ...................................................................5 |
| III | California Times ................................................................8 |
| IV | A Spiritual Lesson ............................................................10 |
| V | Photophobia ....................................................................11 |
| VI | Another Life Outside This One........................................14 |
| VII | Chemotherapy..................................................................16 |
| VIII | Journey With Return .......................................................18 |
| IX | I Owned My Decisions ....................................................20 |
| X | Speak From The Heart.....................................................22 |
| XI | Back To The World..........................................................24 |
| XII | Every Life Event Furthers Our Being................................28 |
| XIII | The Meaning of The Crab ...............................................32 |
| XIV | Between Courage and Hopelessness ..................................34 |
| XV | The Body Evolves.............................................................39 |
| XVI | The Art of Doing Nothing................................................41 |
| XVII | Medicinal Herbs...............................................................43 |
| XVIII | The Good Deal ................................................................45 |
| XIX | The Body Burns ...............................................................47 |
| XX | Love Must Be Practiced Like a Religion ...........................49 |

| XXI | Awake | 52 |
| XXII | Going Home | 54 |
| XXIII | The Goal is to Re-Adapt | 58 |
| XXIV | A New Beginning | 61 |

Epilogue ................................................................................63

*I came out of my mother's womb naked, and
I'll return there the same way...*

## THANKS

Gratitude is the gateway to spiritual depth and I now I express it to you:

- To all my friends and family who carried me from the beginning to the end of this odyssey.
- To those who stayed close to me and offered love and affection and that divine energy called prayer. Your light was present and it broke all barriers. Your energy will be with me until the end.

# PREFACE

## *An accepted pain*

When I was 20, I was born into a new life and given a second chance. This may sound strange to you, but in reality it's not: We constantly experience life and death, renewing ourselves daily in mind, heart, body and spirit.

At 20, we are not the same person we were in childhood, or in early adolescence, nor will we be like that 20 year-old in old age. Everything changes, and then changes us. Even though pain is harsh, it also awakens our spirituality and makes us grow.

In suffering, death is present; but after we die, we later resurrect. Christ serves as the profound example: the resurrection will enlighten us in a multiplicity of ways.

My personal story is not only about cancer. Instead, this is a revelation, a calling, a spiritual awakening – a story where a life is broken, only to be reassembled later, piece by piece: Just like the physical body of Christ that was initially shattered and later resurrected to eternal life.

# I. AN ENCOUNTER WITH REALITY

A black cloud suddenly overtook my eyes, my mind, and my body. It was as if the light switch for the world had short-circuited and all the terminals within my body had melted. I suppose this was the moment I lost consciousness. But here's what I recall:

It was an ordinary winter morning. One of those perfect mornings rounded with beauty. A true "California morning" with bright blue skies, but eerily little noise. It was also one of those mornings like so many others – as I stood holding a pan by the handle, cooking for the family Flores, with their beautiful children in front of me. Yet, one does not equate braking shells and beating yolks into salt and pepper with the "melting" of the physical body.

But that is what happened. I melted into the ingredients that stood in a tall line on the bar, next to the crockery. And that's where the kitchen ends and the next world begins, as desperate screams tried to encourage me to return to myself – with the hustle and bustle of white coats and masks, of stretchers and sirens pulling me back.

"Miss Mercado!" Miss Mercado! Can you hear me?" The paramedic shouted while nurses tried to find my pulse that barely clung to my weakened body. "Miss Mercado, do you know where you are right now?" He asked again, without me knowing for sure.

How could I know where I was? An unknown man was speaking to me from behind his medical mask. No one from the La Familia Flores was anywhere in sight, and I was not in the kitchen cooking their food.

"Miss Mercado!" he insisted, ordering his assistants to take blood samples and check my pulse and vitals. "You lost a lot of blood and are in shock. Do you have any idea what happened? What is the last thing you remember?"

"How should I describe the scene in La casa de la familia Flores to a stranger?" I asked myself. How do I show him the daily scene and the routine?

"You are in the hospital, you've lost a lot of blood," he repeated, convinced that I wasn't going to answer him.

Finally, I responded through weak breaths: "I was making breakfast at La casa de los Flores; "I should be there now. "What happened to me?"

"Its too early to tell," he said, trying to reassure me. "That's why we're going to send you to another hospital for more tests."

As he spoke, I could hear a nurse in the background calling the ambulance. "You don't understand! I need to return to the house and continue my duties," I said, clumsily trying to explain my circumstances. Despite the situation, I believed that the family would be waiting for me.

And then suddenly a siren sounded – it was my ambulance, and the sound transported me to the morning when I first set foot on the ground in California. In hindsight, I imagine the sirens and the riot of ambulances reminded me of the danger inherent to East Palo Alto, where my older brother and his wife lived.

I arrived to their house and they welcomed me with open arms. Instantly, I saw a new chapter of my life beginning. At that moment, the episode seemed impossible to imagine as part of me was still there in the land I'd left behind. They say God works in mysterious ways. Although

I'd heard the phrase uttered many times before, I never understood its true meaning until I reached Palo Alto.

My brother – "Maestro de Ingles" – and his wife had only been married for a few months and were expecting their first child. They lived near the parish of San Francisco de Asis, which became my refuge as I adapted to the new world and its new people and the odd language they spoke.

Paradoxically, the church was a symbol of birth and death for me: Although I wasn't aware of it, I was dying. My soul agonized without me being fully aware of what was happening. Buried feelings yet to be revealed boiled inside me – like the magma that waits patiently under ground and then flows forward at just the right moment.

Feelings. Emotions. Traumas. Frustrations. Disappointments. Broken promises – everything was rising to the surface now in one big fiery ball. Finally, that ball was uncovered one day unexpectedly via the collective voice of the choir group in that church to which he belonged.

I was welcomed into the church community with open arms. From the onset, it seemed like a family reunion was taking place in an environment that I could trust. For me, church symbolizes a safe and comfortable refuge where one can feel at peace despite the adversities of life. In this church, I was provided with the support and peace of mind that a young foreigner needs as she adjusts to a new language and county.

As soon as I crossed over that threshold, I felt part of *something*. I felt welcomed, accepted and supported. Yet, as usually it happens, I was soon reminded me of my status as an alien in the very house where I resided. One day out of he blue, my brother and sister-in-law informed me that I could no longer live with them. I didn't know the reason why they made the decision, but that's the way it was. That's just the way life is – one day we are in a place and the next we are called to move our life in a different direction.

Nonetheless, the time I spent with my brother and his family was valuable, and I departed their home grateful for their gestures and for the time they took to teach me about the U.S. A. culture. In hindsight, their choice to have leave their house changed the course of my life. In hindsight, they offered me complete autonomy and freedom and the the chance to open my wings and fly....

# II. THE DIAGNOSIS

Now back to the surreal sound of sirens. No 20 year-old can imagine starring in such a scene. The voice of the paramedics, the hustle and bustle of the ambulances, the lights of the city, none of these images are part of the imagination of any young woman who has just taken her first flight on her own.

"Miss Mercado?" The phrase flooded my thoughts, while the masks and other hospital instruments became adornments for my body. Meanwhile, all of these strangers tried to keep me conscious so that I wouldn't get lost in the abyss of these foreign "streets" – in their danger and coleanonymity.

"Miss Mercado?" It was as if my last name and my age and were my only identity as I wheeled from one hospital wing to another on stretchers. Again I was migrating, and again I did not know the conditions I was facing.

Could this scene be real? Absolutely not! Yet, it was. And as I pondered this, a paramedic pricked my vein with a needle for what would be the first blood transfusion of many. In the blink of an eye, w e arrived at Stanford Hospital in Palo Alto and I was taken directly to ICU – seizures and restricted blood flow to my brain had complicated a dangerous situation. Moreover, my immune system was incredibly weak and I was separated from the rest of the patient population to avert a life-threatening infection. everyone.

"Do you know why you are here?" A doctor with a kind voice asked. "Mmm, no,: I replied, demanding to know when I could go home.

It's almost impossible to describe the the doctor's expression as he took me by the hand and smiled – it was one of those smiles so gentle and poignant that it announced the bad news all by itself.

"You have cancer in your blood," he told me as kindly as possible, "your bone marrow isn't working properly – it's called leukemia." He paused and looked at the hospital walls, searching for words.

"How much do you know about leukemia?" He finally asked, searching my eyes for what he had been looking for on the wall seconds before.

Suddenly, I remembered the stories of the soap operas that my mom used to watch on TV back home in Mexico, remembering the face of one character who died of leukemia.

"I know that people die when the have that disease," I told him. And he smiled compassionately.

"Not everyone dies, medicine has advanced a lot, and currently there are treatments to control this disease, he said. "There are two types of leukemia – chronic myelogenous and acute lymphocytic. The particularity of your case is that you suffer from both."

Tears welled up in my eyes with such force that it seemed as if I had never cried before. Suddenly, I was crying with such force that I saw it as both a protective shield and an escape. As I cried harder, I couldn't breathe; a deep anxiety overtook me and all I could think about was death.

"Do you want us to notify your family?" The doctor asked.

-"Do not!" I yelled out. Even though the doctor and I were speaking, I was visualizing myself prostrate, surrounded by tubes and unable to fend for myself. The image itself destroyed me – I had imagined I would live forever and now I wouldn't even make 25.

"Why?" The Doctor insisted.

"I don't want them to worry about me," I added, not truly understanding the magnitude of the problem. Deep down, I suspected that my circumstances would not matter much to them. My heart hardened at such a thought and I decided to distance myself further.

# III. CALIFORNIA TIMES

*The road to hell is paved with good intentions. – Popular axiom.*

The weather here is strange. Additionally, I was also a stranger to California cartography, which made life for me even more confusing. When I left my brother's house, the pain was mixed with the awkwardness as I struggled with the distance of being so far from home. Now, I am not referring to the walls or the ceiling, but to a *home* which is built from intangible materials – namely, love affection and understanding.

Immersed in these thoughts, I arrived at the Flores house. It was only a few blocks away from my brother's residence, but the change was substantial; little by little, the nostalgia for my family and friends was left behind in an incomprehensible corner of the memory. I don't know if it was my work schedule or a defense mechanism that I'd activated, but life suddenly filled me with new responsibilities that occupied my entire being. My schedules were packed, so taking care of basic needs like sleeping or eating took a backseat. I slept four or five hours and often skipped meals.

In the Bible studies, the liturgy made it abundantly clear that service was the main object in life. It doesn't matter to who or how much you give, all that matters according to scripture is service and giving – this is the only thing that brings us closer to God. Yes! Give time, affection, money, attention, give *everything*. But receiving is never mentioned. It was as if reciprocity does not exist. Additionally, the *self* is not addressed either. Thus, for these reasons, I never thought I was also important. Again, according to the scriptures, Christ expects of us to give ourselves and ask nothing back.

At that time, I believed that to be true. Perhaps it was was due to an erroneous interpretation of the biblical texts, or because I heard the concept referenced so much I was unable to detach from it. *Be a doer and do not stop for anyone or anything*, was the mantra I lived by, since he who does not live to serve is not fit to live. At least this was the immovable doctrine I imposed on myself.

But what about the being and the self? That was a question that had no place in my thoughts.

How many times have we gone through life like this? Focusing all our efforts on others while ignoring our own needs. At the time, we feel invincible, as if the power of service is a true superpower that makes us unbreakable.

As I developed my *be-in-service* attitudes, I became popular and respected in the community, which inflated my spirit and made me feel needed. And I must confess: sometimes I thought these acts were bringing me closer to sainthood.

But I will tell you share a very sad truth: nobody teaches us to stay with ourselves, to serve ourselves. When I tried to gain self-awareness, I found that I was alone. Alone and away from completely away from *me*. Yes, it was true that in my days of service I found an escape from my other longings. Nevertheless, the loneliness that motivated me to dedicate my life to others was also bringing me further way from my core.

# IV. A SPIRITUAL LESSON

Sometimes a series of circumstances come together to forge a person's character and bring meaning to his life. That was the great lesson I learned during those many meticulous days of service. In fact, I was so absorbed in channeling my own needs into helping others that I didn't realize I was falling victim to a grand ego trap.

You might wonder, how is this possible if I was neglecting myself? Well, the ego can be a monster that feeds on illusions, destroying the essence of our identity. Simply, my identity was being lost among the illusions of the ego as I waited for the next thank you and pat on the back.

In hindsight, I thought I was actually capable of rescuing the world. But from what? It turns out that each person is their own savior; remember, not even Christ himself could save those who were not prepared to listen to his message. Even though Christ's word has prevailed throughout the centuries, even he is was capable of that level of magic. Sadly, it is not possible to save those who have closed their eyes, ears, lips and hearts.

Nonetheless, I naively believed that I could alter this fact. But in reality, I could not, and I almost died trying because I didn't know how to hear the messages from my own heart. Even though I participated in the pain of others, I did not understand it. And all I ended up doing was ignoring my own pain which eventually brought me to my knees.

# V. PHOTOPHOBIA

*People don't really want to be cured,
what they want is relief.*
**Anthony de Mello.**

This anxiety, this cold desperate urgency, began to invade me. I needed to find relief, I needed a band- aid to cover my pain – not because my body needed it, but because I wanted to get back to my work and the arduous mission of "rescuing others".

But I was still in shock. Eyes wide open, yet dazed, I listened to the words of the doctor. And when spoke, he filled my head with unknown terms, with words that seemed to come out of an encyclopedia and that paraded through the corridors of the hospital like so many shadows. The doctor went on non-

stop: Informing me about procedures and care, about pills and treatments and care protocols, about doses and quantities and schedules... everything was mixed in my head in a mad scramble with only one goal – *health*.

At one point, the doctor addressed chemotherapy: "This treatment option deploys a chemical assault on the cancer, with treatments designed to fit individual cancer patients. This is not 'one-size fits all' medicine. Instead, each case is different and medication is prescribed according to the disease. To make chemotherapy more effective, we consider your weight, your height, your medical history and the intensity of the condition. In the beginning, we will start with a single dose and closely monitor how the body reacts..."

Every word the doctor added to his explanation made everything sound more confusing to me. I felt lost as they moved me to a cold, dark room; I was certain that this was going to be how my future looked. In this new room, more problems surfaced: I continued to lose vaginal blood, and this caused a second blackout. The doctors controlled the situation with medication and I woke up dizzy from the sedatives.

"You lost consciousness due to bleeding," the doctor explained when he saw me awake.

His words were meant to be kind, but how do you kindly tell someone that their body is giving up?

"We wanted to control the bleeding, but we couldn't do it unless we gave you a contraceptive pill," He asserted. "We had to wait for your priest's authorization to proceed because you're Catholic."

I met his words with sorrow and some anger. He must have been ashamed of his behavior – stopping to assess religious rules while risking my life in a new way.

-"Why did you do that?" I asked angrily. "I should have given the authorization, it is about MY BODY."

"In the registration forms you indicated that you are Catholic, right?" he asked, trying to justify his motives.

"Yes," I replied dryly, openly showing indignation.

"Catholic people do not accept the use of contraceptive pills, they say that it is a sin to use them," he argued. "That's why we had to make that decision and wait for your priest to give us permission to proceed."

"Doctor," I reflected, "I'd like to make some changes to the registration forms. I don't want there to be misunderstandings of this kind in the future, because confusion like this can kill me."

With that, the nurse quickly left the room, returning a few minutes later with new forms for me to sign. He put them in front of me and asked me which parts I wanted to modify.

"I will erase that I am Catholic. I also don't want to specify race or ethnicity, please leave everything blank," I requested. "I'm just a citizen. I mean, one more person here in the US."

It seems incredible now, but these changes helped the doctors proceed with greater freedom going forward. Suddenly, they understood that it was essential for me to save my life without proving my beliefs or my ethnic origin.

Since that day, I have reflected on the obstacles that can arise through these labels and the difficulties that hundreds of citizens – especially women – can face in a life and death situation like the one I had been thrown into.

# VI. ANOTHER LIFE OUTSIDE THIS ONE

At that time, youth group projects thrived. The events came in a whirlwind: Weekly meetings, Christmas plays, Saturday choir practices, and general church services, in addition to readings, Eucharist and activities for young people. Given all that was going on, weeks were incredibly short.

These activities, and my membership in the group, gave meaning to my life. I dare say he was happy.

But when I look back now, the time and energy I invested coincided perfectly with the verb "to do." I was not completely alive, for part of my being remained in a dusty hidden corner – almost an illusion. Without really knowing how it happened, my life became monotonous. In reality, I was an automaton repeating the same movements over and over again – perfectly fulfilling a function, but without an independent person. In the end, all I was doing was serving and entertaining others.

He had many friends. And somehow, I became everyone's lifesaver. "You need something? Talk to Fel," was the common refrain among my acquaintances. And that's what they did. I used to search my book of resources for tools through which to provide support. I did it all: back-up support; the perfect listener; the adviser with just the right word, the friend always ready with a a hug someone else needed. Just like that, my name became relevant, and I became popular. Ultimately,

I surmised, this is what God wanted from me and I should abide by that and want the same.

Love also fell into the background. If I couldn't even love myself, how could I love someone else? Thinking about a relationship was something that did not figure into my scheme or schedule.

But life is quite curious. And among his great curiosities, the Creator put an angel in my path. An angel whom I will call Fernández...

# VII. CHEMOTHERAPY

I like to think of life as a garden. Or like a farmland where one plants seeds for harvest in the Fall. Sometimes the fruits that we collect are amazing, but their quality often depends on the care we provide throughout the process.

Fernández was one of my two great and closest friends when I fell sick. Looking back, I see that I met many good-hearted people, people dedicated to community and ecclesiastical service. Fernández came from a very religious family, so he joined the group with great enthusiasm. Both of us worked hard in service, and he eventually became my right hand.

Fernández came to the hospital as soon as he found out what had happened to me and he refused to leave my side. He was attentive to the detail of my every need, taking care to involve himself in my circumstances. The hospital became his home during my stay and even after I was discharged, he stayed close by and took responsibility for my care.

Generosity often manifests itself in such complex situations. I imagine if affection runs deep deep it will invite an expression of gratitude. Latino people grow up in the midst of a culture that teaches us to value such gestures. We are told that friendships show "through thick and thin," but until you are thrust into such a radical situation, the meaning of those phrases does not become tangible.

My first chemotherapy was a complete disaster. My body refused to take the medication, seizing up and shutting down, putting up a barrier against the drugs. My body went of my control, growing forcefully disobedient. Even the doctors didn't know what to do, while the leukemia continued to progress at warp speed.

In turn, they doubled the dose. And when the last drop of medication entered my body, I felt death, losing a piece of my life. The last image I recall before the blackout was that of the IV pushing the medicine into my right arm, the scene taking place without my order or authorization.

The medicine hit my blood stream, and my body lapsed into a coma.

# VIII. JOURNEY WITH RETURN

The cracks in the room and all its pores began to light up. A dense whiteness sprouted from the walls and began to cleanse the environment. It was a full-bodied light, almost a fog. But rather than blocking my vision, as usually happens in mist, this thick wall allowed me to see everything – all the details were magnified; it was a true epiphany.

And just like the light, my body floated through the atmosphere across the room. I was detached from the bed and from everything, suspended in mid-air; I was enveloped in a lightness that only freedom is capable of granting us.

So I felt free. Free of what? From fear, from obligations, from constant dedication, from my regrets. This light was a visible manifestation of freedom, and it touched me with its particles. It was the light that raised my body, and I could look down on the room that transformed into another place: My body flew to an alternate plane and everything we know as earth became a tiny dot below me. I had never felt so free or so safe.

And while I journeyed onward, my mind conferred with Him. With Him, who is up there and takes care of us, enlightens us with his grace, with his wisdom. That's when a beautiful truth was revealed to me and it gave my body a new breath of life. The light, that light... was

Him. His hands, his strength, his infinite wisdom. He spoke to me, but without a voice, and he caressed me, via unfading particles of hope and consolation.

That light touched my heart, my sick body and it told me: "You are going to be fine, you don't have to worry." As he made me feel those words, he deposited me back onto the hospital bed.

This was God speaking directly to my soul.

# IX. I OWNED MY DECISIONS

It would be impractical to try and describe in common language what happened that day. Instead, I will attempt to describe the totality of the experience that made me see life differently. This journey was detached from the mechanisms of reality, yet nonetheless still inhabits my memory as a tangible "fact.

The coma state is said to represent a total absence. Those of us who experienced it were not *there* at all even though we were *present*. And therein lies the paradox that led the doctors to think about the possibility of disconnecting me.

In literature, the word 'sublime' refers to experiences that are both terrifying and beautiful, describing those moments when light and shadow converge and are equally beautiful and powerful. I see the moment akin to an electrical storm that we cannot stop looking at it: even though danger is ever- present, we remain enthralled by the lights that adorn the sky.

It would be unfair for the people who stayed around me in the hospital to tell them that I was on a trip where I found myself in a different way. They did not know that I saw them cry and could perceive their sadness and concern. And how could I ever explain to a doctor that an event classified as medical had a greater impact on me on a spiritual level?

Doctors later told me that I was "absent" for three days. I can imagine their anguish n not knowing what to do or if they should disconnect me. But in the end, this was not not their place; I had full custody of my body and life.

At the hospital, they called family and friends and updated them on my circumstances. They let them know that what was happening was unusual. They said my case was unique case and that they didn't know how to proceed. While I remained comatose, others wondered if they should make decisions about my fate, struggling over whether I should live or die. Yet, because I had fought for autonomy, I owned that decision alone; it was out of everyone's hands but my own.

# X. SPEAK FROM THE HEART

"I don't understand your cruelty! Your decisions are not fair, nor your actions, nor your facts, nor anything! Why, God? Why do you take away righteous people? Why despite his love for his neighbor, his dedication, giving us so much of himself? Why her who dedicates her entire life to others and to your own church, God? Why are you taking her? Why now that I care so much... now that I found in her a different human being and after we have managed to connect? Why so, God? Does your cruelty hurt her and hurt me too? How do you expect me to believe in you after these acts of cruelty? I'm sorry... but I can't believe in a ruthless God."

After saying these words, Fernández burst into tears. It was cold on the roof of the hospital, above he fifth floor. The city looked different from that perspective. I am not referring to the night or the cold, but I am referring to the moment when you think you are losing someone who brings a trace of hope to your life.

Perhaps Fernández had imagined a life by my side. Deep down, his rage spoke of love and he felt abandoned by God. Yet, who am I to judge his weakening: Who has not denied his benevolence at some time in his life? And who has not wondered, in those darkest moments, if God is really there for us? It is a natural, human question that haunts each of us.

From the fifth floor, Fernández saw life come and go in a single moment. And he turned to the one who could most understand his rage: God. He waged war against what he considered the greatest of injustices, shouting until he burst into tears.

But after he wept, he calmed down. He breathed until he felt calm, until his pounding heart slowed for a moment. Suddenly, he was able to think clearly again. He looked into the soft California sky again and redirected his words to God. This time they were no longer filled with anger, but instead were kind and compassionate:

"God, I am not the one to reproach your decisions. You win. If you want her to be with you, take her. There is nothing I can do. But listen to this, if you leave her with us, I promise I'll take care of her until the last day."

After saying these words, Fernández felt an almost immediate relief in his heart as woman's voice responded; and this voice said: "She's going to be fine." At that moment, he turned to look at the city from above. The lights that returned to their customary brightness. After I had recovered, Fernández told me that it was the Virgin of Guadalupe who had spoken in his ear and relieved his fear.

# XI. BACK TO THE WORLD

I recovered my sense of hearing first. It's been said that when we sleep the senses are disconnected. Then when we wake and return to the world, we do so through sounds. In Mexico, the roosters crow very early and begin to warn us that the day is starting again. Little by little, they enter though our ears until they manage to make us open our eyes. After we are conscious, we feel the sheets (touch). Next, the sense of smell awakens via the aroma of grass, flowers and coffee. Finally, there is taste as we savor the stews that serves as the cornerstone of the typical Mexican breakfast.

Thus began my return to the physical world: I began listening to the natural sounds of the hospital – the quick steps of nurses and doctors who run to save lives. This blends with the sound of the many surnames that are called with desperation – "Miss Mercado?" And this blends with the incessant ambulance sirens outside. How many people like me were recovering from a short *absence* at the very same moment? But in reality, a three-day absence is not really short for those who on the physical plane like Fernández.

But not all the sounds of the hospital are dark. The laughter of the nurses can also be heard as they plan to go party after their shifts. And the happy sound of parents visiting a newborn baby were most remarkable as new life was welcomed into the world.

As I returned, my ears had a hard time getting used to this grand mixture of sounds. Some stunned me and others were comforting. And then in the distance, I heard Fernandez's voice:

"I think it moved! Nurse! Nurse!" he shouted insistently. "She shook her head! I think it means something!"

"I'll call the doctor," the nurse answered, equally moved by the event.

"Feli, do you hear me?" I could feel him touch my shoulder, and then my arm ever-so-gently, with the care that only nurses know how to demonstrate.

"Fernández, talk to her so she can recognize your voice," the doctor said when he reached the room.

I could hear everything, but there was no way to communicate yet. My body still wasn't responding to my commands, even though I remained there in the midst of the people who had been fighting for my life. I heard and felt them, I even saw them! Yes, from that other plane to which my body floated. I could see everything: every movement the doctors and nurses made as they checked my pulse and charted my temperature I witnessed. I saw every crack in the room, I noted every corner. Yet, I wasn't there physically and there was no way for them to know my exact condition.

And then everything suddenly fell silent, as if all hope had been lost. It was as if the movement that Fernández had observed had simply been a false alarm, just some trick played on him by his own mind that was so desperate for me to return.

They were all about to leave the room again, and that's when I began to cough: "Water!".

"Water!" was the first word I said. My first breath of life and my first contact with the world demanded water. Water" that colorless, odorless liquid that always connotes life.

My throat was parched and I felt like I was dying of thirst. My body demanded that I hydrate it as my senses tried to connect more clearly with their surroundings. Even though my eyes were open it was as if I were somehow still absent, unable to see anyone. All I noted were ere silhouettes, were shadows moving around me. Some objects and faces began to reveal themselves more clearly and were completely new to me. It was as if I had never had contact with them (or was discovering their existence for the first time). Even my own hands seemed foreign to me now, as if they had never belonged to me before (or, better yet, as if they were a new gift from God).

"Do you know where you are?" the doctor asked with urgency. "Can you tell me your name?" he insisted.

Between his voice and the silhouettes, the questions resonated inside my head, throbbing deep inside of my consciousness. But can we call it consciousness? At that moment, I was in the transition phase, in between the unknown plane and this physical plane on which I had lived my life. It was as if I was crossing the border and migrating again; but this time, my journey was more powerful because I was coming back to life. On that day, I truly understood the meaning of the word *resurrection*.

"Can you hear me?" the doctor's voice insisted, far and near at the same time. "Do you know what day it is today? Who is the president of the United States? Do you have family? Where do you live?"

At some other time, these questions would not have seemed strange to me. But on this day, they struck me as odd as I struggled to re-emerge into the earthly world.

The doctors and nurses rechecked my vital signs without me being able to answer their incoherent string of questions. In turn, they spoke slowly to me, knowing that I would not be able to understand their words clearly. They also explained what had happened to me.

But I will be honest, I didn't understand much of what they were saying. I just smiled ever-so-gently. The truth was that I had just returned from a trip that had left my soul perfectly calm. And I didn't want to do anything to disturb that serenity.

# XII. EVERY LIFE EVENT FURTHERS OUR BEING

As noted on its website, the Stanford University Medical Center is a world-renowned facility comprised of multiple hospitals and clinics. It has continually ranked as one of the best hospitals in the world for both instruction and patient care.

Historically, the site has healed millions of people – including myself. In the future, it will heal millions more. God showed me his generosity by putting this hospital near me, guiding me to specific hands. I was diagnosed and healed there. Specialists in oncology were present, in addition to hematologists, psychologists and some medical interns who observed my case as part of their studies.

During clinic, we sat in a circle so that I could see everyone and everyone could see me. I was the case study and I was there to tell my story, providing my history that would help experts outline the reasons why I now suffered from this strange disease. The doctors, holding notebooks and pens, stethoscopes around the neck, were there to eagerly to find out what had happened to me. They asked about my previous symptoms, about my habits, about the place where I lived. And I told them the whole story:

"It all started with a cold. It happened just like other common colds – slight body aches, sore throat clearing, nasal congestion. But the difference between this and other colds was its duration. The average cold last 2 to 5 days. But this cold lasted forever – one week went to a month. And still I was down.

Suddenly I realized that I had been sick for a long time but hadn't paid careful attention to it. How could I care about a cold with all my business? I didn't even have time to reflect. I just took over-the- counters medication and went on working.

But then I noticed that I had bruises on various parts of my body. Nonetheless, my life was so busy I failed to appreciate the gravity of the situation that had evolved. When I discovered those initial bruises, I naively assumed that I had bumped myself. As I spoke, the medical crew recorded every detail in my description. And in their faces I noted concern. It seemed inconceivable to them that I had not taken these symptoms seriously, yet they did not say that aloud. Doctors are ethically trained not to judge patients, so they stayed in their roles.

"Where do you live?" one asked abruptly.

"East Palo Alto, near the PG&E power plant, I said, narrating my story. "I have lived there one year and see the plant from my bedroom."

They asked me to try to remember other strange events, other symptoms that my body had manifested. So, I forced myself to remember.

Days before my menstrual cycle that month, I had an episode of chills and sweats that warns the body that a bad cold is coming. A cycle with intense bleeding followed. When I recalled this fact, the doctors took immediate note, as a piece of the puzzle fell into place.

It's incredible how we normalize what we don't want to think about because "we are too busy with our work and with our obligations." Thinking in those terms, we exploit our own bodies endlessly. Now I know that I should have listened to myself more, but in those days, I couldn't stop myself. I couldn't put my responsibilities aside because of a cold or a menstrual period, no matter how unusual the events were.

Looking back, my menstrual bleeding was always heavy, so I didn't give the event much weight, although I was aware that it was much more than I was used to. I just carried sanitary pads and went about my life.

"At the Flores house on the morning I fell ill, the children were waiting impatiently – I had promised them a special breakfast and they wanted it now," I told the doctors. "The rest of the story you already know..."

The doctors listened attentively to my story. They took notes and examined documents in unison. "You just described all the symptoms of leukemia, including the environment in which it grows," one of them said, his voice serious and his brows slightly furrowed.

"I'd like you to explain more about that," I told him impatiently.

"Leukemia is known as a type of cancer that forms in the blood stream," he added. "Sometimes it can be caused by things s present in the environment. Like from a power plant."

The medical interns and I watched him closely as he spoke on.

"The cancer takes over the bone marrow and the lymphatic system. There are many types of leukemia. Some occur especially in children and others manifest only in adults, as is your case. In such a case, the white blood cells act as the defenders of our body. But leukemia affects the way white blood cells are produced, so that they act abnormally and divide chaotically."

"Are the symptoms I suffered due to that?" I interrupted.

"The symptoms that you just told us are exactly those that derive from this condition – fever, chills, constant fatigue, weak body, common infections, weight loss, swollen lymph nodes, enlarged liver and spleen, bleeding, bruising, red spots on the skin, excessive sweating at night, pain and tenderness in the bones. This is an attack on the system from both the outside and the inside. But, since we are not trained to identify it, we do not immediately realize the danger we face."

The doctor went on to describe how the symptoms manifest. He narrated some clinical cases detailing how other people got sick and what they experienced. Finally he said that the fact that the fact I lived so close to the power plant had definitely contributed to my illness.

"Is that the cause of my illness?" I asked.

"We don't know for sure, but it's consistent with the onset of illness," he said. "There is literature on external factors such as a power plant causing this disease. The truth is that leukemia does not have a specific cause, it is not hereditary, nor does it happen from a specific event. We don't really know the reasons why cells stop working properly."

"Why me?" I asked. I thought I had spoken to myself, but I asked the question out loud. The same question that I had been asking myself for weeks kept echoing in my head and in my heart to which there was no answer. The silence in the room made that very clear to me. None of the doctors present dared to even try to outline an answer, and deep down I knew that one did not exist.

At the end of the interview, most of the doctors and interns left. Only Dr. Greenberg, the psychologist and myself remained in the room. The psychologist suggested I take a therapy session weekly to help me cope. I accepted, but I only attended a couple of times – I was just to sick to do more.

Dr. Greenberg told me that my coma had given them all quite a scare. H e said that my case was rare and I struggled to find hope in his words. It seemed to me science really did not know what to do. He offered me options and ideas, ranging from taking a new combination of drugs to waiting for a bone marrow transplant. In any case, there was nothing more I could do personally other than keep the faith. So I accepted everything the doctor proposed, and intense chemotherapy sessions began.

"Let's do it," I told him, unsure of where I was being led...

# XIII. THE MEANING OF THE CRAB

The history of disease is fascinating if we look at it from the outside. Disease and death have been been the subject of various books in philosophy and science since the dawn of man. As humans try and explain the reasons for their frailty in words.

To this day, no one has discovered the specific cause of cancer, which seems as unique as the individuals whom it afflicts. However, the trait all diseases shares is found in its ability to shake us from our comfort zone and make us acknowledge the death process. There is palpable fear when someone says "I have cancer." And it takes an almost unbreakable will not to give up, while that same question echoes over and over again – *Why me?*

Like Doctor Greenberg, I, too, was scared. I was especially heartbroken and couldn't understand why things were happening the way they were. Additionally, my body showed side effects from the coma. But thankfully, it remained strong enough to fight against the chemotherapy.

Chemo-therapies are strong medicine and they kill all the cells in the human body, both the bad ones ("the invader cells") and the good ones. On one hand, the body is healed; and on the other hand, it is made sicker by the cure.

Both modern medicine and ancient wisdom say that you have to learn to listen to your body. My body was in pain. So much so that it reacted in unexpected ways. Suddenly, it began to communicate, telling me that what was happening was only the beginning.

The set of drugs that they gave me were relatively new I was a part of a clinical trial; it short, my body was an experiment at Stanford Hospital on which the brightest doctors in the world were testing their theories.

Every drug that they gave me had horrible side effects, but the doctors kept saying the reaction is "normal." But what is "normal?"

One of the thing the doctors did was go slow. Every time I received a new medication, I had to be rushed to intensive care, where the doctors had to figure out the cause of the sudden adverse reaction. I was living in a nightmare. Strictly speaking, everything had turned into a strange nightmare – I lived in a state of perpetual lethargy from which only the pain that assaulted body could penetrate.

Anyone who has ever been a patient in a hospital knows perfectly well these are not *friendly* places, even if they do house an assortment of friendly doctors and nurses like the ones who cared for me. In reality, hospitals are cold and rather inhumane places where the the human body becomes a walking "experiment" – the patient dehumanized in favor of science. This is what happened to me, and it changed me forever.

# XIV. BETWEEN COURAGE AND HOPELESSNESS

During those moments, I felt abandoned, orphaned – first by my body, and then the outside world. In light of the excessive invasions of my body by doctors and the news that there was no suitable bone marrow donor, I felt completely alone. Not even my brothers and sisters were compatible donors, and this left me out of options. How was it possible that even flesh-and-blood relatives were not compatible with me?

There is no way that a person in my state could understand it, so I tried to find the answers in the only one who knows everything: God. Yet, apparently he didn't have answers to give me either, because I gained no enlightenment. Being helplessness is unbearable, especially when it comes accompanied by the news that it's you're going to die. Being forced to say goodbye to the world and everything one loves and knows is an impossible task. *Why me?* That was my favorite question, and I clung to it at all hours like a mosquito clinging to fruit.

I was furious with everything. And, without knowing why, I was also angry at myself. Days passed and grew furious with animal rage; it was if my subconscious was incapable of explaining things to me. Silence roared from every corner.

"Why is that, doctor? Tell me why?: I demanded. I lost count of the number of times I asked the same question without hearing an answer from anyone.

"Patience, Miss Mercado," Dr. Greenberg used to tell me.

"How do you expect me to be patient under these conditions?" I asked, reproaching myself silently.

My health, my body, my entire circumstances now depended on assistance from others. The person who had the least control over my actions was me. Given this mess, how does a person not feel anguish, frustration, pain, anger and anxiety?

And then the inevitable happened: I started losing my hair. I watched it fall away from me as I ran my fingers through it whenever a visitor appeared. And I saw it on the pillow when I woke up from deep dreams. And I saw it slide off down my body and clog the bathroom drain, mixed with tears. Suddenly, I didn't want to look at myself in the mirror because, by doing so, I would come face to face with the reality that hurt so much to see. That's when I would catch my reflection in other faces – and it was something that was utterly impossible to see.

"Could you please bring the razor?" I told the duty nurse day in a fit of painful resignation.

"Are you ready, Miss Mercado?" she asked, knowing that I had refused to shave my head days before. "I'm ready to shave my hair completely," I answered very quietly.

He nurse immediately retrieved the machine, returning with it hidden under her arms. After years of working in the hospital, she obviously knew the pain I felt. And then she looked into my eyes and moved the corners of her lips slightly. I felt her words crash: It's for the best."

"Ready?" she asked again in a sympathetic voice.

"Yes," I replied, tilting my face so she wouldn't see me cry. But it was unavoidable.

"I'll start at the front," she told me. She made a move to start the job, but stopped abruptly and sat down next to me, touching my chin to comfort me. And then she started cutting my hair, from front to back. I felt how easily the machine moved since there weren't many strands left in its way. As the machine moved across my scalp, sparse strands fell here and there, next to my feet, across the nurse's shoes. In between, my tears kept falling.

"Don't worry! You're going to look great, you'll see," she told me. "Besides, your hair will grow back soon."

*But what it it didn't?* I wanted to ask. In my head I asked the question, and if it was as if the nurse could hear me think.

"You are so beautiful. It will grow back."

Although they were the right words to say, my body was not listening, my mind was traveling to the unknown noticing everything and nothing in reality nothing really matters, at that point who cares I should be focusing in getting better not in how I look…Forget about vanity that does not exist here, perhaps the creator was telling seek vanity within not outside of you but at that time that was not the case I wanted things to be the same like they were before. Who was I kidding life does not change it never sits still, I needed to die to be alive, I needed the darkness to see the light, I needed the road of the cross to resurrect and shine.

## Chemo Process

(during)
The chemo process
(idle)
With cancer
(wore)
Hats knitted close
To the skull
(hide)
The loss
Of hair
(watching)
Naked blue leaves
Shiver blonde
Against the fangs
Of wind
(watching)
That immaculate moon
(move)
Imperative with urgency

(there):

Old man
Sam Sanders
(closes)
His cafe
(fiddling)
With his

## FELI MERCADO

Pants' pockets
(turned)
The chairs
(up)
Side down
(on)
The tables again

**By John Aiello**

**January 1, 2009**
**Lafayette, California.**

*\*Writ on walk with Feli, New Year's Day, 2009, after discussing the idea of suffering with unnamed angels.*

**© John Aiello: 2009 & 2022. All rights reserved:** *No part of this poetical work may be reproduced or transmitted in any form or by any means, electronic or mechanical – including photocopy, recording, or any informational retrieval system – without written permission from the author.*

# XV. THE BODY EVOLVES

The way I looked that morning after the nurse left the room was an omen of things to come. As I saw it, my body was wasting away, transforming into an unknown entity. Not only did I lose the hair on scalp, I lost the hair on my entire body – on my armpits, on my pubic area...everywhere.

In retrospect, it was a kind of flashback. Suddenly, I saw myself as a little girl in Mexico running from one place to another wondering what was going to become of her life. I also saw the awkward adolescent who struggled through puberty unaware. And again, I felt like that: Naked and and not knowing exactly where I was going with a body that was transforming against my will.

I already knew that chemotherapy was a violent treatment, but only understood it after it was used on me. My own distorted image told the story as my dreams disintegrated in the mirror along with this painfully skinny body. It may sound strange, but when I saw myself I resembled one of those round and yellow Popsicles that I ate during my childhood in Mexico. In my dreams, my body appeared as a nightmare coming from within – it was as if another being now inhabited me. And in those dreams, a shadowy figure spoke to me, revealing that the speaker was in fact me.

"You are not me! I'm not me!" I yelled, slapping the shadow away. Sometimes I woke up repeating these same words. But was it really me? Was I lying to myself?

As I grew sicker, all of activities and physical needs required external help. In addition, I my legs didn't respond to brain commands and I required a wheelchair. It seemed that even my limbs had rebelled against me and I was no longer unstoppable. Now my languid legs reminded me of my vulnerability, my fragility, my helplessness. Even though I couldn't moved, I fought even harder, determined to say strong, determined to live.

How did I know to fight? I suppose that when the body remains wounded, the mind that takes over via thoughts and ideas and dreams. And, of course, via internal dialogues with God. If his plan was for me to be like this, then that is what I had to do – remaining as calm as I could while the movie played on...

# XVI. THE ART OF DOING NOTHING

Suddenly, the wheelchair became my ally. It was my mode of transportation, my ticket to see the world that existed outside the four walls of my room. When I needed to breathe fresh air and look at the sky, when I needed to feel the sun on my skin I took to my wheelchair and away we went.

It's amazing how the gifts of nature are missed when you enter "treatment." At Stanford, I felt isolated from the natural world. Every time I went outside, I had to cover myself up because my immune system was weak. I had to wear masks and use all kinds of filters and devices (placed around my body, my arms and my head) which prevented kept germs out but prevented me from breathing properly. Now, finally out in the open air, I reflected and tried to dialogue with Him in peace.

My diet was also strange: it consisted mostly of liquid vitamins that entered into my system intravenously. This is how I survived, since the smells and flavors of real food made we vomit. And who could be hungry? In the midst of chemo, my body couldn't tolerate any type of food. Every day was the same – from dawn to dusk, I lived medical treatments and even emptied my stomach without having filled it with any food.

It is incredible now to think that this was my life for almost three years. My life was and endless parade of doctors taking notes and me asking questions – of them an myself, asking God why he was making me go through so much suffering/ I didn't understand what the point was. I did not understand what I had done to deserve this fate.

On more than one occasion I asked for it to be over. I asked Him to take me, to cut the thread of life because I couldn't find enough reasons to live this way. Perhaps I didn't have enough energy to even consider the possibility of going on. It was simply too much for me. I'm sure it would have been too much for anyone, because what life or what human being can be prepared to go through such an artificial process?

But was it a test from God? If so, it seemed excessively harsh. One day, a friend from the youth group came to visit and brought the Bible with him, and insisted that when I was ready I should read the book of Job.

"Perhaps reading it will give you a little more encouragement," he said, leaving the book behind on my bed.

# XVII. MEDICINAL HERBS

And then someone came to see me. A person capable of traversing the halls of the hospital with her powerful voice and steady steps. A person to whom I have been united from the first moment of life and whom I always carry in the sweetest place of my heart. A person who was able to calm my body and mind and put an end to the medical coldness with her reassurances. Only one woman could be capable of these things – my mother.

She arrived loaded down with medicinal herbs she'd brought from Mexico – remedies that could help me withstand the cruelest moments of pain. My mother is truly a "Mexican mother from before." She is steeped in traditions and the old ways, often unpredictable in her demeanor, sometimes confused by the American customs. But she has always strong and committed to her children.

In the old Mexico where I grew up, love is not shown with sweetness or tenderness. Instead, affection is hidden somewhere between scolding and guilt, hidden in simple actions and messages that slip away like poetry on deaf ears.

My mother arrived in Palo Alto with plants from Mexico meant to cure me. Her visit was an act of unmistakable love. As were the reprimands she subjected me – strings of questions merging into accusations that this was somehow my fault because I didn't obey and did everything alone. Even though her words stung, I listened to her with my head down, searching for love between scoldings.

My mother used her power to demand action from the doctors, demanding that I be made more comfortable. In turn, the doctors attended to each of her requests, somehow making herself heard despite the fact she did not speak English. A true "mom," she there for my relapses; she was there when a fungal infection attacked my lungs and my brain; she was there when they cut my body for endless biopsies; and she was there to demand clarity from the doctors about what could happen to me in the process.

It was at this moment in time when my lung collapsed: In the aftermath, I woke up trembling in pain and despair, staring at the ceiling, waiting for the wound to heal. Mom was also right there when a treatment they gave me went awry and there when an infection caused a stroke. And she stayed at my side when the MRI tube made me claustrophobic.

Yes, my mother came from Mexico and stayed, watching her defenseless daughter cry the baby she'd carried in her arms decades before. And in that same way she was there to defend me from the world called "Stanford," rescuing from my pain. In her own most poetic way, my mom went through cancer right along side me.

# XVIII. THE GOOD DEAL

I could go on narrating my mother's exploits in the hospital for 100 more pages, because they are definitely linked to my recovery. As I look back, I see that her strength extended to me. As I look back, I admire her bravery, admire her daring to fight authority and confront the endless line of doctors when things seemed wrong to her. I also admire the stealth she showed when cleaned my body and spread ointments on me, giving me Mexican medicinal herbal teas to drink.

And my mother's will made me see that I wanted to live! Undoubtedly, I wanted to live, and I was fighting as hard as my body and heart would allow. And when I felt completely down, I thought of the good things in my world – as I thought of the loving people who were around me, I fought to survive. That's what fed me hope and gave me strength.

The medical team that treated me was unparalleled. In their hands, I felt safe and they encouraged me to continue fighting. Still, scientific knowledge is not always synonymous with human knowledge, and one day, a doctor on my team encouraged me to die peacefully at home. In this doctor's eyes, my efforts no longer made sense. Perhaps this doctor's opinion was steeped in the scientific method and made sense to them, but to me it sounded cold and sterile. Where was the human care? What about my dignity? I was told sternly that death was inevitable and that the best thing I could do was go home and spend the last days of my life there. I won't deny that I almost believed what I was being told. Close to giving up, I cried with eviction, as if my departure from the world truly seemed imminent.

I suppose that such awareness is necessary, however. None of us will live forever, and the exchange with this cold doctor reminded me of human fragility and the transient nature of life. The exchange also reminded me that I was a fighter who was choosing to live a little beyond cancer. It's almost like this doctor made me promise myself that I would live. And then, like another angel, my mother appeared again, demanding that I be treated with dignity. Mom narrated the facts of what had happened to others on the medical team and they asked the doctor who'd told me to throw in the towel that they should withdraw from my case. When this physician received the news, they expressed surprise, warning me that I would never survive without their help.

Looking back now, these events encourage me to reflect again about words and attitudes, reflecting on how the things we say impact others on a life and death level. I hate to say it – but that doctor's words almost defeated me, while my mom's actions actions made me see a light again. Tender and kind people are necessary: they fill us with goodness, and inspire us to offer dignity and humanity to others.

# XIX. THE BODY BURNS

The doctors weren't giving up either. In unison, they kept practicing, trying to figure out ways to help me survive. At one point, they suggested a lumbar puncture. During a lumbar puncture, a needle is inserted in your lower back between two lumbar vertebrae and a sample of cerebrospinal fluid is taken for analysis. Cerebrospinal fluid surrounds your brain and spinal cord and protects them from injury. A lumber puncture can help diagnose serious infections, such as meningitis; disorders of the central nervous system, such as Guillain-Barre syndrome and multiple sclerosis; as well as cancers of the brain or spinal cord. Additionally, a lumber puncture is performed in order to inject anesthetic medications or chemotherapy drugs into the cerebrospinal fluid.

The lumbar procedure was one of the most painful treatments I would endure. I found the pain unbearable as it placed my body is a completely vulnerable state. The puncture actually made me burn – inside and out. Immediately after the needle went in, my body temperature rose to an unspeakable level: 104°F (40°C). I was literally burning up and the doctors did not know how to proceed. The searing, merciless pain consumed both body and mind. I felt like I was becoming a monster, shedding my skin, as sores formed. At once, my body changed color. It was all happening before the incredulous eyes of my mother, who washed me with baking soda so I might "heal faster."

\

When a pain of this magnitude takes over the body, time becomes endless, while every puncture to the skin feels like a hot iron that will mark the soul forever.

But in the end, that pain actually disfigured and then rebuilt my body. After the procedure, my regenerated skin felt soft like that of a newborn and the moment became a metaphor for the spiritual rebirth that was to come. Believe it: The body is wise. It is part of nature and, like the wilds, it finds a way to adapt and survive despite our human fragility.

# XX. LOVE MUST BE PRACTICED LIKE A RELIGION

As time passed, a clear light came to this story. My body was slowly restoring itself and the pain was giving way to peace. Slowly, things were changing for the better. In light of this, my parents were about to return to Mexico, since their visas only allowed them to stay in the United States for six months.

At that time, news spread that a miraculous healing water had been discovered in the State of Mexico.

The testimonies from people broadcast on television gave my parents and I renewed faith. Faith is the only thing that saw me through my ordeal. How many times I called on my saints to fight the battle! And it was faith that made me look beyond the scope of medical possibilities.

When we learned of the healing water, Fernandez offered to travel to Mexico to retrieve it, and after three days, he returned with it. I drank it with enthusiasm, but my body rejected it initially. It took many weeks for my cells to accept it.

After months in the hospital, days became difficult. But the company and empathy from the many people who visited me made it tolerable. There was always someone with me: Fernández, mom, dad or friends from church all took their turns staying at my side. We talked and played music, we shared ourselves without restraint. Each visit was a concert that I attended, dressed in hospital clothes and a mask, sitting on my wheelchair. The smiles and conversations of the boys buoyed my spirit and fought off my depression. God manifested himself in those young men, keeping himself near-by at all times.

But calmness doesn't always follow the storm; sometimes, it announces it. The doctors noted that my infection was under control and decided to give me preventive radiation to ensure that my body was completely safe. So one day they transferred me to the Nuclear Medicine Department. Even though the name intimidated me, I called on faith to see me through a new ordeal.

In the Nuclear ward, they pierced my temples and introduced a light probe into my temple meant to burn the malignant cells. But like all cancer treatments, it is an aggressive and punishing on the body. On that first evening after the nuclear treatment, I was taken back to my hospital room. Some relatives and friends were waiting in the corridors. Among them, I saw my mom and dad, waiting for news about my situation. They were the first to find out that I had suffered a stroke caused by that bolt of radiation. And they were the first people the doctors told that I would not survive that afternoon. They were instructed to begin the paperwork for funeral services, since my heart was very weak and could not withstand the defibrillator discharges.

I can only imagine my mother's reaction – her surprise and frustration and anger. She had assumed that the disease was in the rear-view mirror, and suddenly she was told to get ready to buy her daughter. The death preparations proceeded in accordance with our Catholic-based faith: The priest came to anoint me with the holy oils and Fernández's mother gave me a scapular, because it is said that whoever dies with a scapular is guaranteed entrance to heaven.

And while they all cried, my consciousness wandered onto another plane of reality in which I was became an assiduous walker. In this new world, I was guided by sensations, looking to understand and then end my struggle.

The next day I woke up at noon with a headache so intense it felt like someone was pulling my missing hair from my skull. There wasn't an inch of my head that didn't hurt, and no one to tell me the reason by body revolted in the manner it did.

# XXI. AWAKE

I would later come to understand that these relapses would become the normal reaction in the months ahead. Although I often became excited about the positive results and the good news, there were countless ups and downs that also followed. I spent a year hospitalized next to six other cancer patients. Although all seven of us had a similar diagnosis, my case was unique due to the number of unexpected reactions I experienced. These reactions led the doctors to experiment with various treatments and sometimes these experimental medications did not work. Even today, some 30 years later, I find it hard to understand why everything was so difficult for me. How was I supposed to deal with the pain? What was the purpose of my circumstances? What was I supposed to learn?

After that nuclear-related relapse, they told me that I should spend at least another four months hospitalized, but my body and my spirit only to take three of those months. One morning, a doctor came to my bed to talk to me.

"Everything indicates that your platelets and your immune system have been stable," he said. "Now we must wait for your appetite to return; if the number of platelets increases, you could leave soon."

"Understood doctor," I replied, happily imagining my return home. But to which house would I go? And how soon?

As I said before, I had to becareful not to get my hopes up too high. Set backs were common-place for me, and I was getting tired. Moreover, my appetite did not return, and each attempt to eat food was accompanied by pain and vomiting.

"Why don't you use marijuana?" a nurse suggested when she saw that my daily life was falling apart.

Fernandez and I were surprised at the proposal, especially since it was illegal at the time. Nonetheless, I tried it, taking two capsules of "Mary-Jane" right off the bat. Surprisingly, after three hours, I was desperately hungry. I ate as much as I could, but shortly after, my body rejected it and I vomited. But at least it was a beginning. My appetite had started to come back and over the following weeks I made progress.

Finally, one morning, my team of physicians – psychologists, nutritionists and oncologists – evaluated my condition and gave me a long list of instructions that I had to follow to ensure my recovery. The first and most complicated on that list was that I had to return to a sterile environment. But my reality was bleak: I had no home, no job, no money, nothing. Thus the idea of leaving the confines of the hospital represented unspeakable anguish juxtaposed with elation.

And if this "push and pull" between excitement and terror were not enough, my body revolted again: Suddenly on the eve of my reunion with the world, my cells stopped producing potassium, creating a new roadblock that would delay my exit from Stanford.

# XXII. GOING HOME

Doctors were also dumbfounded by the absence of potassium in blood stream. They concluded that it was due to the chemotherapy I had received. Frankly, I was use to it: this was certainly not the first roadblock I had encountered, and I had grown accustom to the highs and lows. And what I came to discover is that the human body is powerful and resilient, searching for ways to survive.

My mind, on the other hand, weakened, with my thoughts betraying me from time to time. I no longer understood this game of life and I often felt defeated – each disappointment a new hurdle to overcome. But in the end these hurdles marked valuable experiences that brought me back to God and the universe.

At first, I was given potassium intravenously. This kept me alive until I was hooked up to a device that helped my body produce it. For a time, this small machine became my faithful and necessary companion, like so many other machines that had joined forces with my body on this long journey – the needles, tubes, cables and scalpels had become actual extensions of my existence commanded by God. And as much as I denied Him, He was always there helping me to decipher a message that I couldn't see clearly due to the blinding pain.

Two weeks later, it was finally time to go home, or more accurately, to leave the hospital: As I said before, I was homeless and nowhere to go. Suddenly, I saw the world as my "home." The coldness of the hospital and its confinements made me rethink my place in this great collections of planets and sky, of rivers and trees and stones.

"We have a proposal for you, Miss Mercado," one doctor said in a tone that was mixed with authority and shyness. "We want to discharge you to rest and recover at home and we will follow your case closely. This will do good things for you."

The strange box making potassium would go with me. Now it was part of me – at least for a while. We were united by the singular possibility of survival. Even though the reasons were not clear at that precise moment, it was evident that I wanted to live. It I didn't, my body would have shut down. Thus, from that unknown corner of my being my sense of survival was triggered, and I accepted the doctor's proposal.

I left the hospital and went to my brother Bob's house; he had agreed to receive me and he prepared a space for me to be comfortable in a hygienic room that would be accessible to the medical providers who came to visit me.

The staff arranged for me to be out-fitted with a wheelchair and masks; they placed me in the chair and Fernández led me to the electric exit door. When it opened, the wind brushed my body, but I did not feel the warm air that I imagined would embrace me after a year of confinement. Instead, I felt a cold rush and it ran through me like a sharp knife. My aching body put up quick resistance. Three seconds later, I wanted to return to the hospital room. The wind felt foreign to me and the sunlight too much: the incandescent light of the midday sun made me squint hard and after a year of artificial lights turning on and off in a small room.

Suddenly, the world was too big for me – it suffocated me the way the narrowness of four walls would have done at another time in my earlier life. Then came the external noises that I was no longer used to hearing. The time in the hospital made me get used to the sweet voices of the nurses, the hurried voice of the doctors, the firm voice of my mother and the compassionate voice of Fernández. But now the sound of society stunned and startled me. As we drove, the speed of the car overwhelmed me.

I was scared and I wanted to go back. So I closed my eyes like a newborn just seeing the earth for the first time. Certainly, this was like a second birth – coming into the world with that thin gray layer over the face to protect our eyes. We come here fragile and defenseless, hungry to return to the bubble of protection that is the womb. And I needed to go back to my bubble. For months, I longed to get out of the hospital, longing for freedom. But at this moment, the word freedom took on a strange meaning; it was as if it was too big a word for the small entity I had become. Yes, freedom scared me. But who hasn't been scared of being free? Fear is confusing because it can deprive us of our faculties. As I advanced, I had to relearn the basics, changing my place of confinement. I was going from being captive in a hospital to being captive in a house, but at least there I would be surrounded by the warmth of a home, with loved ones there nearby.

And thus began my new life. I am not exaggerating when I say that I was born again. It is not just a metaphor. In reality, I was a baby again. My body, my mind and my emotions all had to adapt to the outside world. As a child, I had begun to move by crawling, and now I looked at life from that exact perspective.

I summarize the months that followed in memorials to my relapses. The ups and downs were like the wheat fields that sway in the strong winds of old Mexico during the month of March. In the wind, some plants break and look for a way to get back up. Others lose their foliage or bend, too weak to continue Others dry up and lose their seed. As in the parable, "you have to die to live."

Fernández stayed with me like a guardian. He walked me through the ordeal, cleaning the potassium machine countless times a day, saw that I ate and accompanied me to get blood transfusions. As the thick blood of strangers entered my body, I realized they also joining my cause, intertwined with my journey. I was one of many: All kinds of people came to the hospital – presenting with different ages, cultures, languages, genders, complexions, and beliefs. Yet, there was a most tangible energy built on hope and faith that united us. Even without ever speaking to each other, we spoke the same language, united in our suffering, fighting to survive. I have no idea how many of the people are alive today, but from the bottom of my heart, I wish they all made it.

As time progressed and I regained my strength, I discovered that my fear of death came from the fact that I felt I had not lived long enough yet. I had not realized my dreams and I was still searching for meaning. In the New Testament, it says that we leave everything behind to be free.

Today, I can say that I lost everything, and that in this way new ideas and new possibilities were born inside me. A visible sign of this new beginning was the hair that was beginning to reappear on my head. There in my brother's house, I sat bare: I had no possessions, nothing belonged to me. I just had myself, my story, and this chance to start over. With everything in front of me, there for the taking.

# XXIII. THE GOAL IS TO RE-ADAPT

When I left the hospital, the people who who were there for my fight were still there by my side. Sometimes they witnessed my progress, and sometimes they saw me stumble. My first new steps were taken alone. My mother was back in Mexico, and the other people who took care of me were back to their daily lives.

As I began to recover, I would see the possibility for a new life. First, my body began to accept solid food and I functioned more safely. I regained energy and the dizziness stopped. And then one day, during the second phase of recovery, my body miraculously started producing potassium again, allowing me to say goodbye to the machine. Suddenly, I had one less thing tying down my life.

After I endured a a slight relapse, my doctors advised me to change my living situation, asserting that the conditions were not conducive to healing. The idea shook me – unless you have been through it it is impossible to describe the feelings of loneliness and abandonment that follow you like a shadow.

Upon hearing this news, Fernandez spoke with his family and they prepared a room for me in their house and the whole family came together to take care of me. If there is a definition of friendship for me, it is called *Fernández*. Furthermore, if there a pure manifestation of 'angels on earth' he would embody that manifestation.

With the third phase of recovery, I suffered more relapses. Even though it was a natural progression, I felt exhausted; I was fed up in the face of pain and I asked Him repeatedly – "why me?" With each new machine connected to my body, with each new wound, my reproaches against God grew louder.

Today, I still have a seven-inch scar on my belly that reminds me of the battles I waged against cancer. And when I touch it I do so with appreciation and with pride, thankful that God let me survive. This scar reminds me that I am strong, that I withstood the cruelest of circumstances and survived. When I look at my story today and think of those scars, I see the first lines that were written on my body. It reads like a narrative. It says all stories matter. And this one is is mine.

This is the story of how the love and courage and the love of my closest allies gave me strength to endure. And this story documents that I was able to see these people from other plane, documenting that I did not want to leave them. Instead, I want to love them and thank them now for helping on my journey.

And this book is a testimony, then, to how I lost everything, testifying to how I was left without any material possessions – the only thing I owned was my life. A fragile, delicate life, but at the same time – a life of strength and determination. And although this is also the story of how I almost lost faith, it is also the story of how my faith was renewed at the darkest of hours as I recovered my health via many miracles.

And this is my testimony to the heroism of others: to the doctors who often lost their way trying to heal me; to the other anonymous patients who lived through immense pain; and to the honor of those that cared for me selflessly.

And finally this story testifies to the grace of Christ. So many times I lost patience and questioned the love of God and my very existence.

But though it all HE spoke to me and pushed me forward. In the end, this story is about His voice speaking to me and giving me back my breath in the face of enormous pain.

One day God appeared before me and said: "Your purpose is not over yet. This is just the beginning. Dust yourself off. Stand up and walk". And that is when, in the midst of the confusion, I recognized my body again, asking Him for forgiveness for having lost my faith in the blindness of my pain.

# XXIV. A NEW BEGINNING

And I called out to God: "Earlier I spoke through my despair and my frustration. I recognized that the pain was greater than me, and that I said things without thinking. But I take back my words now. I had heard of you, but I had not heard or seen you. Now I can see you with my own eyes," I said, fingers intertwined.

I looked at my body as I detached myself. I sat motionless and helpless, fragile and without energy, without reason to live. And I looked at my arms and legs as they vanished. At that point, only the beating of my heart remained close to Him. My heart rate increased and it resounded like an invitation to life. I returned slowly from that dream, and little by little the movements were incorporated into my extremities. I felt the breath in my chest and the fingers tickling my hands and feet. Then I felt life. I was alive again...

The treatment lasted for another two years. The complications did not stop – the pains, chills, and dizziness was continual. Eventually, I even lost an ovary. But life raged on inside of me. Sometimes the events surrounding my life seemed unspeakable to me, however here I am – alive, narrating the story. In the end, all the suffering taught me to live in a new way, in a more loving way, genuine and dedicated to others.

# EPILOGUE

> *"A story is the shortest distance between humans and the truth."*
>
> **A. De Mello.**

This is my story. A story of peace. A story of life and death. A story of rage, love and kindness. A story of madness, frustration and sanity. A story of contentment, enlightenment and darkness. A story of pure life, of abundance and solitude. And this is a story of life and death, without 'good' or 'bad' – abundant in wisdom, teaching through its energy.

And ultimately – this is a story of love. And this is only my story: A story where I experienced being born again, but this time, born while being fully *present*...

When the treatments and visits to the hospital stopped in March 1994, the leukemia was in remission, and returned ti work at the coffee shop where it all started. A few months later, I was hired by a financial institution. I only worked 15 hours a week, but I was able to hone the office skills that my management career in Mexico had taught me. Afterward, I moved to another city and was assigned a new position as an assistant in the operations department of the bank. And then other opportunities opened up for me – everything immersed in light, growth, harmony. And my professional growth continues in to this day.

In the meantime, I continued my personal mission by serving as a volunteer in other organizations. To make a living, I went to work at another financial institution where I stayed for almost 5 years, before being disabled for a year. That disability was life changing, leading me back to school and inspiring me to take my Montessori teaching license. Currently I serve as an instructor and life coach, presenting conferences and classes that invite human beings to create awareness and confront their emotions in day-to-day life. I delight in sharing all my insecurities, processes and triumphs with each of my students. My life testimony is a great lesson that constantly re-educates me and, consequently, enlightens others.

In sum, this is my story and it says that I started living the day they told me I was going to die.

CPSIA information can be obtained
at www.ICGtesting.com
Printed in the USA
BVHW040930300922
648293BV00022B/430